The Colossal Computer Cartoon Book

ORIGINAL EDITION
David H. Ahl – Editing
Pat Holl – Layout
Ned Sonntag – Cover Art

ENHANCED EDITION
Brian Wiser – Design, Layout, Editing
Bill Martens – Production
David H. Ahl – Preface

 Apple PugetSound Program Library Exchange

The Colossal Computer Cartoon Book: Enhanced Edition

Copyright © 2016 by Apple Pugetsound Program Library Exchange (A.P.P.L.E.)
All Rights Reserved.

Published by Apple Pugetsound Program Library Exchange (A.P.P.L.E.)
www.callapple.org

Paperback ISBN: 978-1-365-23488-0

ACKNOWLEDGEMENTS

We would like to thank David H. Ahl for his support and new contributions to this book. Produced in coordination with and permission from David H. Ahl.

Special thanks to the original artists and publisher for this wonderful view into the past.

Cover art by Ned Sonntag.
New Back Cover, Front Cover enhancements, and new Interior pages designed by Brian Wiser.

PRODUCTION

The Colossal Computer Cartoon Book: Enhanced Edition → © 2016 Apple Pugetsound Program Library Exchange
Brian Wiser → Design, Layout, Editing, Art Enhancement
Bill Martens → Production

The Colossal Computer Cartoon Book → © 1977, 1980 Creative Computing Press
David H. Ahl → Editing
Pat Holl → Layout
Ned Sonntag → Cover Art

DISCLAIMER

No part of this book may be reproduced, distributed or transmitted in any form or by any means, including photocopying, scanning, or other electronic or mechanical methods, without prior written permission of the publisher, except in the case of brief quotations contained in articles and reviews.

The Colossal Computer Cartoon Book: Enhanced Edition is an independent publication and has not been authorized, sponsored, or otherwise approved by any institution, public or private.

All images are under copyright and the property of Apple Pugetsound Program Library Exchange, or as otherwise indicated. The original art and cartoons are copyright their respective artists/publishers. Use is prohibited without prior permission.

Apple and all Apple hardware and software brand names are trademarks of Apple Inc., registered in the United States and other countries. All other brand names and trademarks are the property of their respective owners.

While all possible steps have been taken to ensure that the information included within is accurate, the publisher, producers, and authors shall have no liability or responsibility for any errors or omissions, or for loss or damages resulting from the use of the information contained herein.

About David H. Ahl

David H. Ahl is the author of 22 how-to books, including *Basic Computer Games* (the first million-selling computer book), *Dad's Lessons for Living*, and *Dodge M37 Restoration Guide*. In 1974, he founded *Creative Computing* magazine – the world's first personal computing magazine – and was the publisher and editor-in-Chief of *Creative Computing* magazine and six others from 1974 to 1985.

He holds a MS and BS degree in Electrical Engineering from Cornell University, 1961, as well as an MBA from Carnegie-Mellon University, 1963. In 1967, David devised the first computer model for forecasting the success of new consumer products. He has also written more than 1,000 articles on technology, automotive restoration, marketing, Bible, logic puzzles, travel, market research, financial planning and investment analysis. Among computer games, he created Lunar Lander, Subway Scavenger, Orient Express, and 50 others.

David's hobbies include racing 1950s Triumph sports cars, collecting and exhibiting WWII patriotic stamped covers and classic first day covers, and collecting toy tow trucks. He is an award-winning photographer, restores historic military trucks, hikes, and sails. And he is a softball pitcher and coach, collects antique and historic Bibles and leafs, and repairs anything! Read more about David at: http://swapmeetdave.com.

Some of his favorite quotes include: "Learn from the past; live for the future."

"You can never have too many bungee cords, AA batteries, or rolls of duct tape."

"The circles around you can include or exclude ideas, people, and events. Draw large circles."

About the Producers

Brian Wiser

Brian Wiser is a long-time consultant, enthusiast and historian of Apple, the Apple II and Macintosh. Steve Wozniak and Steve Jobs, as well as *Creative Computing, Nibble, InCider,* and *A+* magazines were early influences.

Brian designed, edited, and co-produced many books including: *The Colossal Computer Cartoon Book: Enhanced Edition, Cyber Jack: The Adventures of Robert Clardy and Synergistic Software, Synergistic Software: The Early Games, What's Where in the Apple: Enhanced Edition, Nibble Viewpoints: Business Insights From The Computing Revolution,* and *The WOZPAK: Special Edition* – an important Apple II historical book with Steve Wozniak's restored original, technical handwritten notes.

He passionately preserves and archives all facets of Apple's history, and noteworthy related companies such as Beagle Bros and Applied Engineering, featured on AppleArchives.com. His writing, interviews and books are featured on the technology news site CallApple.org and in *Call-A.P.P.L.E.* magazine that he co-produces. Brian also co-produced the retro iOS game *Structris*.

In 2005, Brian was cast as an extra in Joss Whedon's movie *Serenity*, leading him to being a producer and director for the documentary film *Done The Impossible: The Fans' Tale of Firefly & Serenity*. He brought some of the *Firefly* cast aboard his Browncoat Cruise and recruited several of the *Firefly* cast to appear in a film for charity. Brian speaks about his adventures to large audiences at conventions around the country.

Bill Martens

Bill Martens is a systems engineer specializing in office infrastructures and has been programming since 1976. The DEC PDP 11/40 with ASR-33 Teletypes and CRT's were his first computing platforms with his first forays in the Apple world coming with the Apple II computer.

Influences in Bill's computing life came from *Creative Computing* magazine, *Byte* magazine and *Call-A.P.P.L.E.* magazine as well as his mentors Samuel Perkins, Don Williams, Joff Morgan, and Mike Christensen.

Bill is a co-producer of many books including: *The WOZPAK: Special Edition, Nibble Viewpoints: Business Insights From The Computing Revolution, What's Where in the Apple: Enhanced Edition,* and co-programmer for the iOS version of the retro game *Structris*. He has written many articles which have appeared in user group newsletters and magazines such as *Call-A.P.P.L.E.*.

Bill worked for Apple Pugetsound Program Library Exchange (A.P.P.L.E.) under Val Golding and Dick Hubert as a data manager and programmer in the 1980s, and is the current president of the A.P.P.L.E. user group. He reorganized A.P.P.L.E. and restarted *Call-A.P.P.L.E.* magazine in 2002. He is the production editor for the A.P.P.L.E. website CallApple.org, writes science fiction novels in his spare time, and is a retired semi-pro football player.

Preface

2016 Enhanced Edition

Like most boys who grew up during WWII and its immediate aftermath. I collected stamps, coins (pennies and nickels), and comic books – especially MAD. I was also into electronics and used to go into NYC almost every Saturday to Cortlandt Street ("Radio Row") and pick up electronic war surplus – submarine radios, bomb sights, walkie-talkies, etc and try to get them working.

As I got on with life, these two interests continued in parallel – bizarre, offbeat comics (MAD, Panic, underground comix) and electronics, which of course morphed into computers. I picked up computer programming in college (Cornell and Carnegie-Mellon) and at Grumman Aircraft in the 1950s and 1960s and kept laughing at cartoons and comics from Tintin to Captain America to Iron Man. And I wasn't the only one! A bunch of nutty scientific types put together a great publication back then called the *Journal of Irreproducible Results*. Great fun!

So when I got involved with my first publication, EDU, at Digital Equipment Corp it was inevitable that it carried cartoons – or at least cartoon-type illustrations for the articles. The publication was designed to support DEC's existing educational customers and sell new ones. About this time (1972) I put together my first book, *101 BASIC Computer Games*, and it too had cartoon illustrations for most of the games and a wonderful cartoon cover by Bob Barner. All of which I carried through to *Creative Computing*, the world's first personal computing magazine, which I started in October 1974.

I ran a few cartoons in each issue but as I beat the bushes for suitable cartoons, it quickly became evident that there were

Preface

far more cartoonists (and cartoons) than I could ever publish in *Creative Computing*. I had published a book of computer art, *Artist and Computer*, in 1975, so why not a book of computer cartoons? To publish a reasonable size book (120 pages), I had to broaden the scope a bit to include calculators, robots, and related technology, but eventually I came up with about 250 suitable cartoons and strips. Most of the cartoons were from the early 1970s because in the 1950s and 1960s no one thought there was anything funny about computers at all. I confess, some that I included were marginal at best, and looking back at them 40 years later I scratch my head and say to myself, why on earth did I ever include that?

Nevertheless, the book was a modest success and it did have a second printing with a less controversial cover than the one by Ned Sonntag on the first printing. Okay, 20,000 copies is a long way from the million copies of *Basic Computer Games* but not too bad for a somewhat strange, offbeat computer book in 1977.

Where do I stand on cartoons today? Hey, I still love 'em and, in fact, I'm currently translating a bunch of Herge's Quick and Flupke strips from the 1930s into English. This is quite a challenge because most of the strips have both a visual joke and a verbal pun or play on words which is very difficult to translate from French into English while retaining the humor. You'll find this project at: http://swapmeetdave.com/Humor/Quick-Flupke. And I still love MAD magazine! And Captain America and Iron Man. Wonder Wart Hog too!

David H. Ahl
January 19, 2016

Preface

Did you ever leaf through a magazine without stopping to look at the cartoons? Not many people do. Indeed, some sociologists feel that cartoons are one of the major influences on public opinion. I don't know if I'd go that far, however, I would not argue with the notion that many laypeople get their information about computers exclusively from sensationalist news stories and from cartoons. And just where do the cartoonists get their ideas? No one knows for sure, but it's fairly clear that the cartoonists are, for the most part, outsiders looking into the field of computers. And this look is generally through a peephole or dirty periscope.

So we probably won't get any profound knowledge about the world of computers from cartoons but that's not the object of cartoons anyway. Besides, it's the incongruous, the unexpected, and the surprise connection that makes a situation funny. And there are several hundred of these fresh creative leaps of the imagination in this book.

Ron Anderson, a sociologist at the University of Minnesota, feels that computer cartoons can be grouped into six categories:

1. Humanized computer
2. Computerized human
3. Computer as a beneficial tool
4. Tool evolves into threatening master
5. The dependent computer
6. Computer people and insider jokes

I don't argue with these categories since Ron has studied the subject far more deeply than I have. However, to lend this book some slight degree of organization (many computer people have this must-be-organized phobia), I found it easier to use a somewhat different group of categories from computer dating to computers in the office and so on.

If you read this far, you probably shouldn't have bought this book. The whole purpose of the book is to read the cartoons and laugh or chuckle or giggle or groan. Who ever heard of a preface in a cartoon book anyway? Let's get on with it and have a little cybernetic fun!

May 1977, Morristown, NJ   David H. Ahl

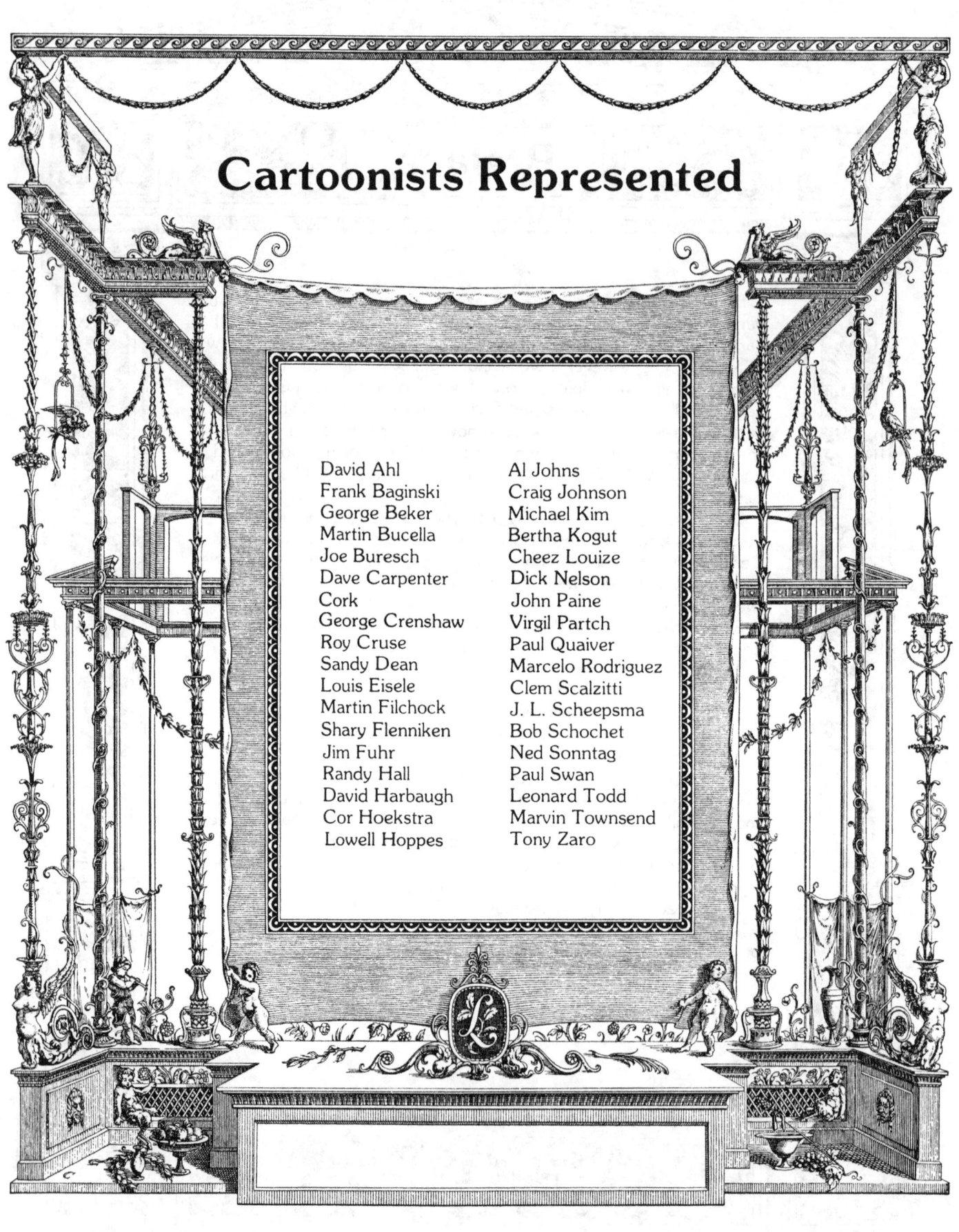

Contents

Lifelong Laugh Lines	1
Think Tank	19
Computer-Ease	24
Amore Potpourri	32
Sandy's Dandies	37
Roguish Robots	44
Inside Jokes	58
Harbaugh's HaHa's	74
Hard(ware) Sell	79
This Does Not Compute	82
One On One	88
Swan's Circus	95
It's Only Human	101
Solo Circuitry	109
John's Jokes	112

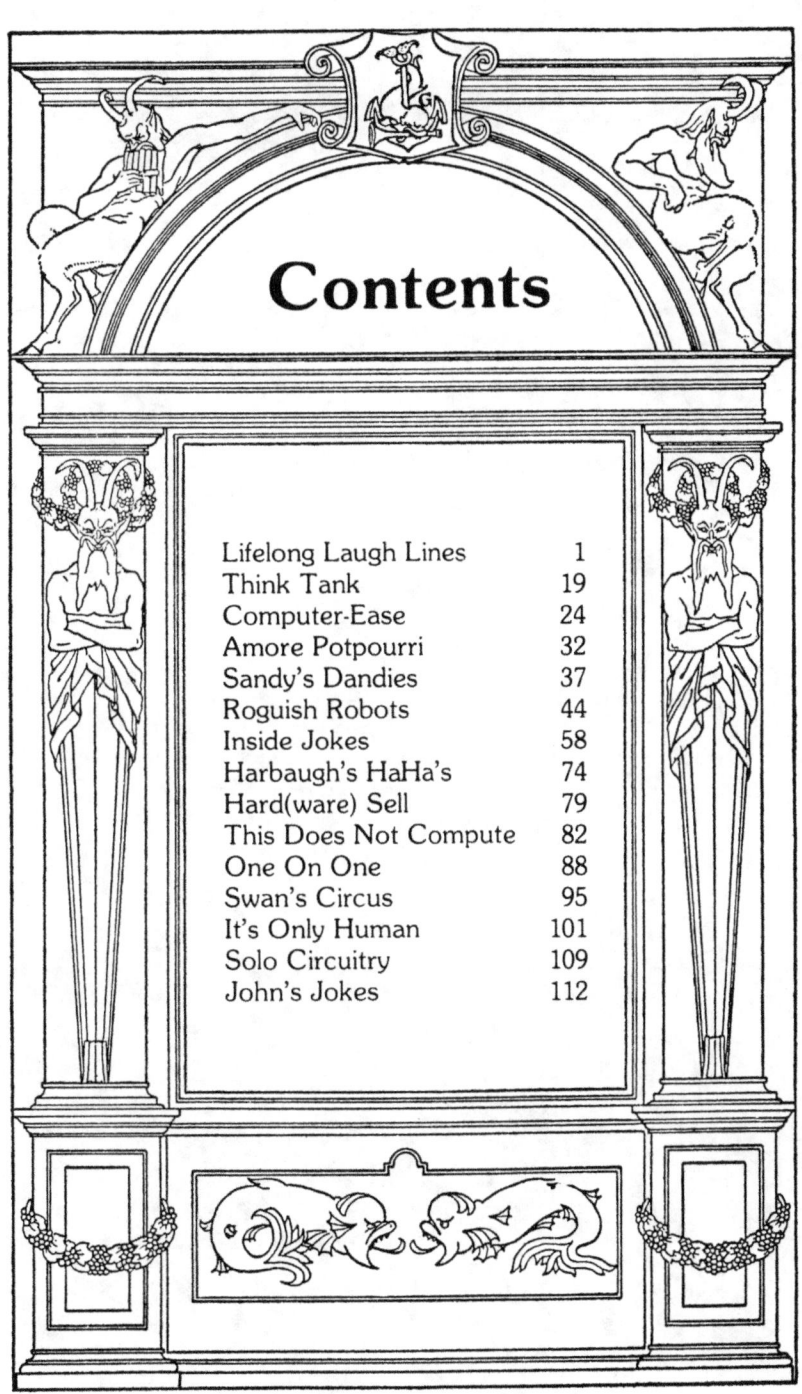

LIFELONG LAUGHLINES ...

"Mr. Hewit, This is your life..."

"Must you always bring your work home with you?"

"I got rid of my computer today, when I decided it could replace me!"

"This isn't quite what I had in mind when I said I'd like to be a game show contestant on T.V.!"

"I'd like a word with your computer."

"I just can't decide which computer is best for me."

"The nerve of them, taking the word of their computer against my pocket calculator!"

"Computer, Computer on my wall .... Who's the fairest of them all?"

"Charlie! Where do you want the computer?"

"Didn't I warn you it would lead to this? First your boss asks you to bring home a little book work, then typing, then a few reports to write up…!"

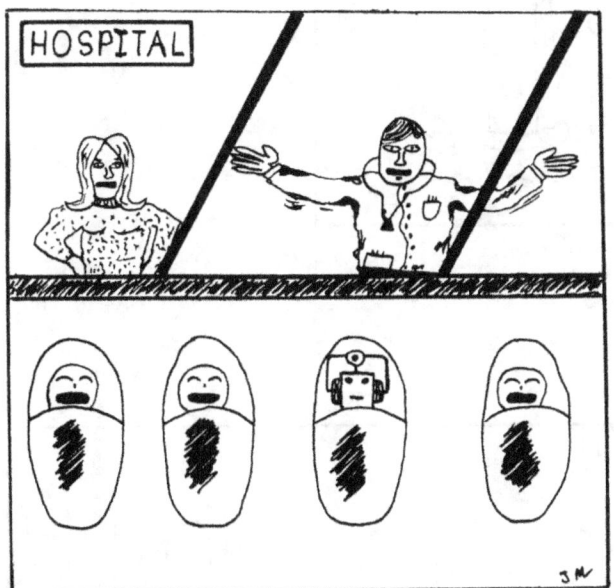

"Mrs. Jones, you have had a most unusual baby!!"

"Poor Harold! He spent hours assembling an electronic songbird and our cat ate it!"

"Wow! The centerfold this month is the new IBM Triplex 304!"

"As you can see, we've programmed the MARK VII with a rather refreshing sense of humor."

"Well Captain Johnson, do you think you can tear yourself away from your galactic conquests long enough to take out the garbage?"

"It's worse than I expected. I've been replaced by a pocket calculator."

"You think you've got problems with a heat sink!"

"Can't you forget business for a day or two?"

"At that distance and location your ball will break sharply to the right .... it concludes with 'Lots of Luck!'"

"What hurts is that I wasn't replaced by a whole computer - just a transistor."

"The housewives are no longer complaining about dishpan hands. Now they've got push-button fingers."

A Creative Computing Exclusive! **SPAN-O-VISION** No. 2

What suspense! Last issue, the massive machinations of Span-O-Vision produced its first VIS-U-COMP rendition, conjuring an unnerving scenario in which computers are nearly rejected en masse by an enraged society, only to rescue themselves with an astounding shift of focus! From the irritation of much misuse and quackery, commercial computer technology developes a pearl:

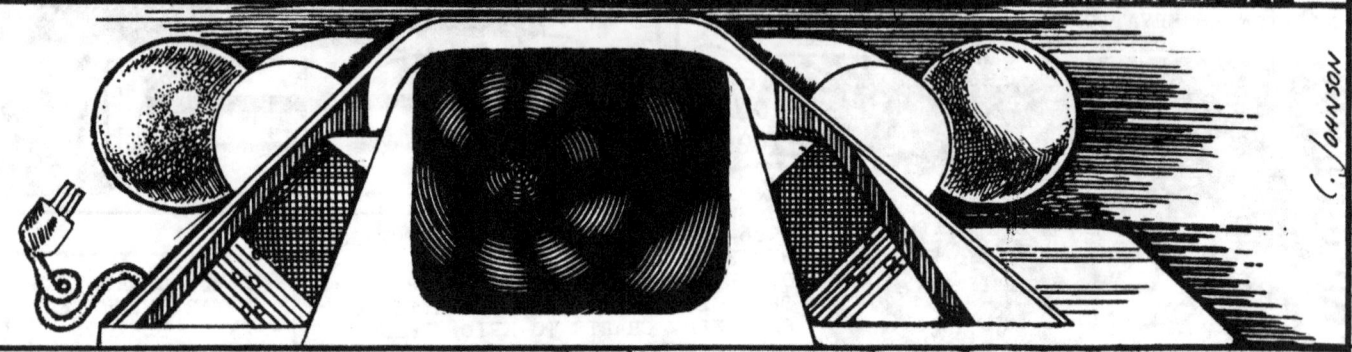

The Val-U-Graph Generator!

This device enables a home viewer to perceive when someone on T.V. is telling the truth! A special PSYCHOLOGICAL STRESS EVALUATOR UNIT reads variences in voice frequencies, determines stress, computes, and signals when a person is fibbing! Feb. 1987- Panicked legislators rush a bill through Congress prohibiting its use in legal proceedings and bans direct judgement of utterances on T.V.

Undaunted, commercial interests and T.V. industry backers devise a prime-time series in which politicians are invited to debate. Computers are programmed with all pertinent information. The debator's voices are fed into the PS Evaluator, and converted into graphic images, colors, and simultaneous electronic soundtrack based on voice frequency modulations!

AND NATURALLY, IF I AM ELECTED, I CAN ASSURE THE AMERICAN PUBLIC.....

...THAT THEY WILL BECOME THE ULTIMATE FACTOR IN GOVERNMENTAL DECISIONS.

[TILT!]

> It is then the task of viewers to debate the credibility of the speakers from evidence within those images (by predetermined criteria)

Gosh! But amazingly, there's more. The home viewer may then extract claims of politician, punch into home terminal linked to huge atomic-powered ENCYCLOTRON (a SPAN-O-VISION evolvement) and receive a brief cinematic scenario immediately following said claim, along with its probability rating! Once again the world is safe for democracy.

"Feed that to the computer and see if it's a message, or just a forest fire."

"I give up. I haven't won a hand all evening."

"How did things go at the lab today Dear?"

"You can start packing Ethyl... My new cyborg is almost done."

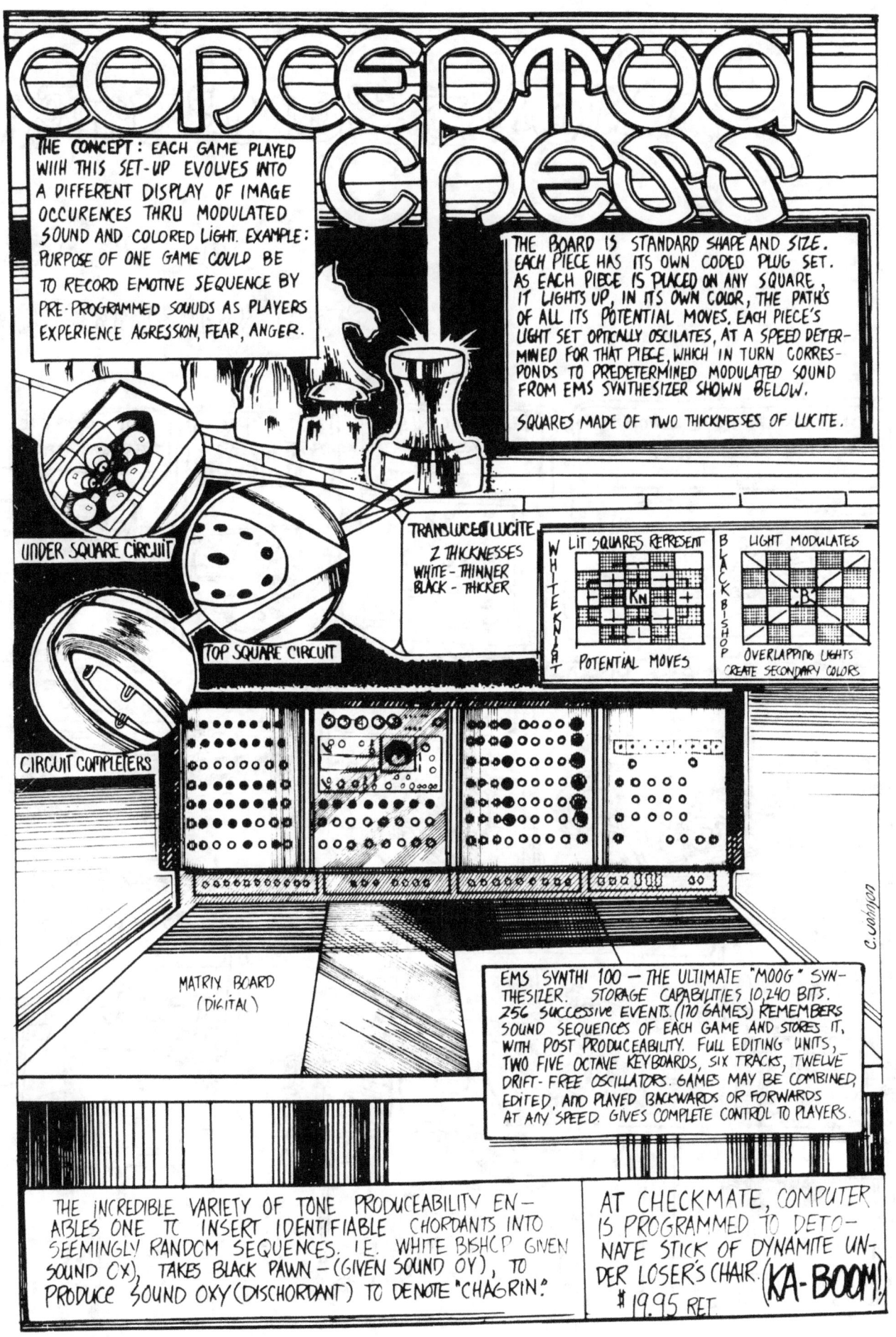

A HOME COMPUTER

as seen by GEORGE BEKER

THINK TANK

"I call them numbers, you can add them, subtract them, multiply them, divide them ... find their square root..."

"I didn't understand all that stuff he said between 'Good Morning, Class' and 'That concludes my lecture for today'."

"Why do I have to know math if I have a mini-pocket-calculator?"

"...No thanks, ... just scanning..."

"You're the Wizard of Oz?"

"But I thought the New Math was done by computers!"

"If it was mine, I'd pin-stripe and wax it!"

"Before attempting to determine the country's next president, I suggest you try something comparatively simple, like who the class president will be!"

"...T12X31LC, this is A561205,LC4A ... I have to make pee pee..."

"We got the afternoon off: Our teacher's been recalled for repairs."

COMPUTER-EASE

"Of course, he wants something that won't fall apart first time he uses it."

"It makes the job of keeping tabs on everyone a lot easier."

"...We'd like to put two bucks on 'Happy Daddy' running in the seventh today..."

1970 –

1980 –

1990 –

"To what do you owe your great wisdom and knowledge?"

"Looks like it might be a nice day tomorrow!"

"Yes, progress is wonderful. This little baby only set us back $75,000.00 and we replaced a $90-per-week clerk with it."

"Let's see now ... Have you had any previous experience with electricity?"

"Any other experience besides selling programs at the ball park?"

"You say you're an expert on computer technology?"

"The computer is guaranteed for fifty thousand miles or until it malfunctions... whichever comes first."

"Not only does it give a more accurate reading than a crystal ball - it doesn't break into a thousand pieces when you drop it!"

"This is Mom."

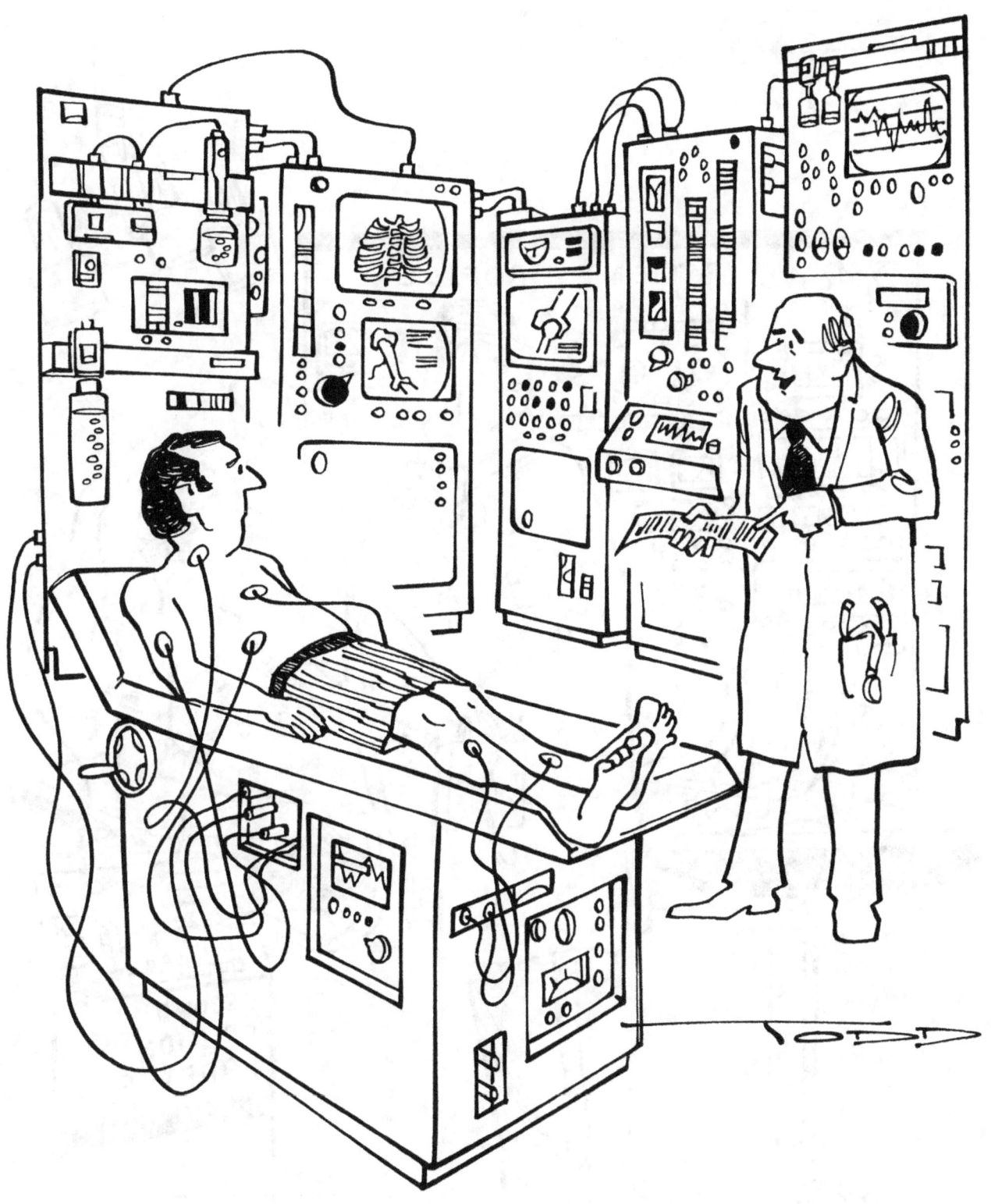

"Thanks to advanced technology we can start treating you immediately ... for either one of five things!"

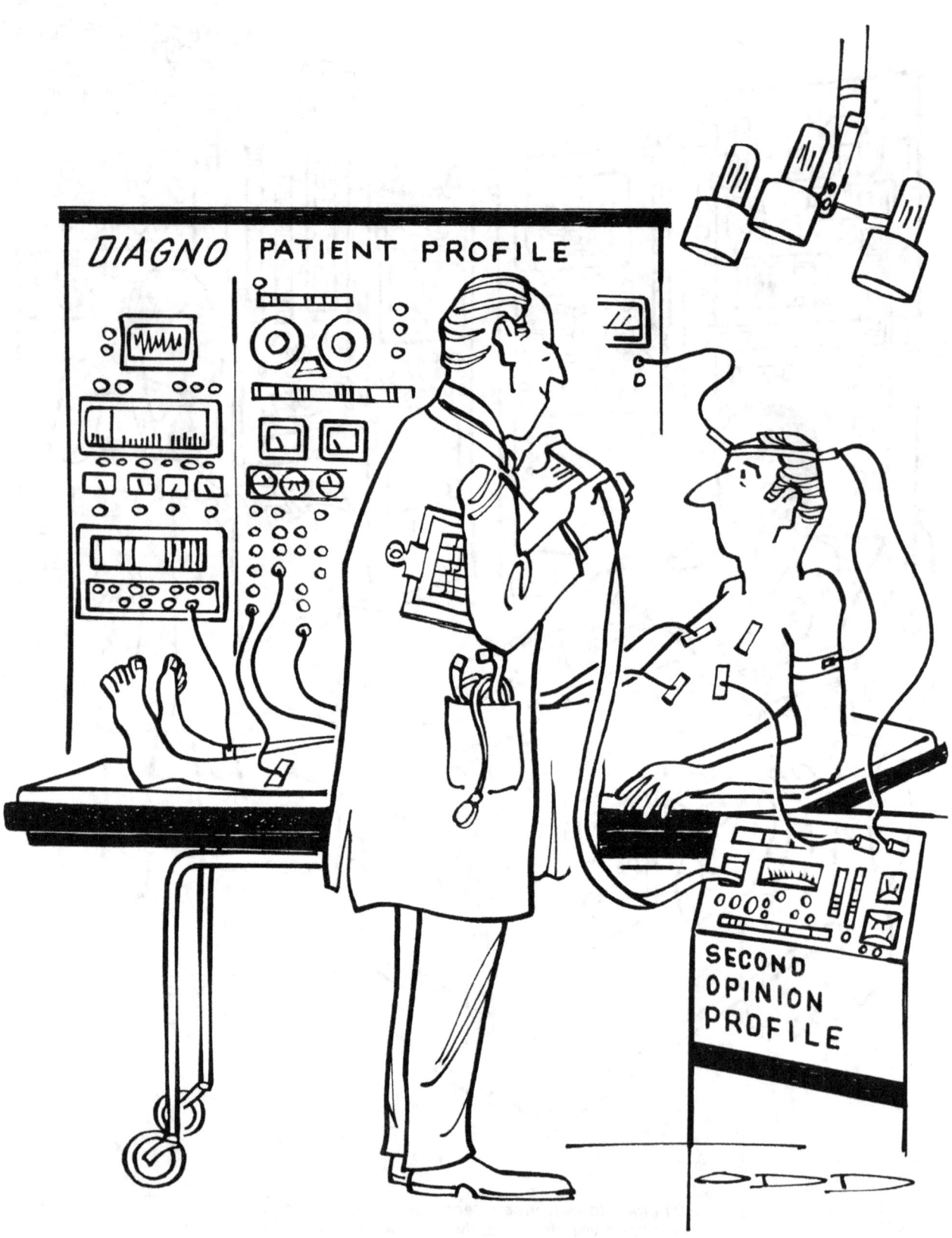

"Right Chief, we're running the suspects through the computer right now."

"He was a top programmer until he fed the machine everything he knew."

AMORÉ POTPOURRI!

COMPUTER DATING

IF AT FIRST YOU DON'T SUCEED, TRY, TRY AGAIN

LOVERS LEAP

SCHOCHET

"Let's not rush things now, Miss Jablonski."

"To think I needed a computer to find you!"

"I think I forgot to tell the computer that Bambi is a Great Dane."

"Cinderella and the Prince could have made it a whole lot easier on themselves if they'd used computer dating."

"Do you mind if I take her outside first and see how she looks in daylight?"

"Gee! my first computer date! I wonder what he'll be like?"

"What could I do? They said the computer never makes a mistake!"

SANDY'S DANDIES

"Yeah? Well, it doesn't make ME feel lowly and insignificant."

"Blast! Those kids have been monkeying with the circuitry again."

"See? It refuses to compute when the Bionic Woman is on..."

"I've got the Acme people on the line. They say they are sorry but your kit contained instructions for a KI-8 kit and you bought a KP-2 kit. They hope you have not been inconvenienced."

"We can't do business after all ... my computer isn't speaking to your computer."

"Honey, were you saving this for anything special?"

"Do I remember what special day this is? Hmm... Of course! It's Norbert Wiener's birthday!"

"Do you suppose my problem could be that I accidentally left them in my pocket and they ran through a complete wash and spin-dry cycle...?"

"To err is human. To really foul up a computer takes a man."

"Shhssh! Hold it ... let's go someplace where we can be alone..."

ACME COMPUTERS

"He said he overheard two of our salesmen talking about the need for debugging..."

"Naw, I don't watch those bionic people TV shows. They're all a bunch of crock. Don't you agree, Ms. Ledbetter?"

"Get the programmer back here! He's crossed the merry-go-round with the rocket!"

"That does not compute. That does not compute. That does..."

"Now hear this! I am the programmer. You are the programmee!"

"What good is our new 50 million results per second when our best operator is hunt and peck?"

ROUGISH ROBOTS {and other super-heroes}

"My programmer doesn't understand me."

"See? The ex-14b is just as agile as any man."

"I compute therefore I am."

ELECTRONIC COMPONENTS

"Never mind the sack; I'll eat 'em here."

"My life has become a dull endless cycle of programming and reprogramming."

"A box of CMOS please. He gets terrible migraines when he has to do intricate figuring."

"DESTROY!"

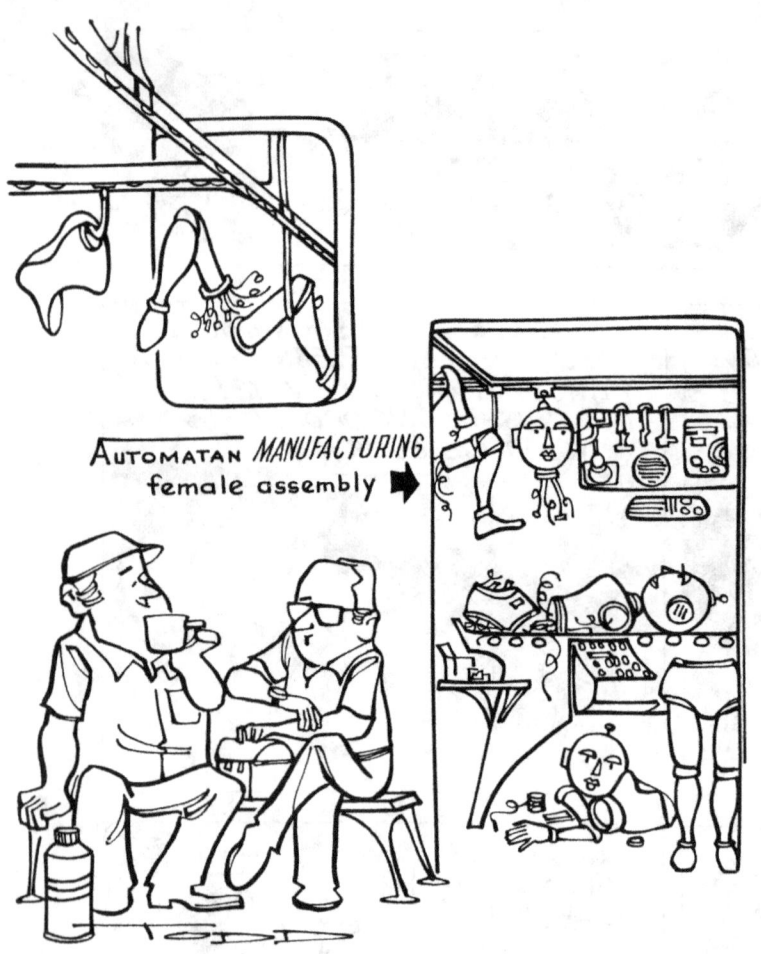

"12:45 Ed; shall we go back in to join the ladies?"

"This is our thinker model."

COLLECT 'EM!

Cut out these cute lil' critters along the heavy black line. Color with crayons, water colors, or "Flair-" type pens. Paste on walls, notebooks, IBM machines, etc. Or make a really keen mobile!

Talkative Terry Telephone

COMPUTER

Freaked-out Freddy Flip Chip

Cyrus CRT

HOURS OF FUN!

Pester Program Bug

LOADS OF LAUGHS!

CRITTERS

Punchy Paper Tape

Dancing Danny DECtape

SWAP 'EM!
Be sure to collect the whole set

THE NUTTY PROFESSOR'S NUTTY ROBOT

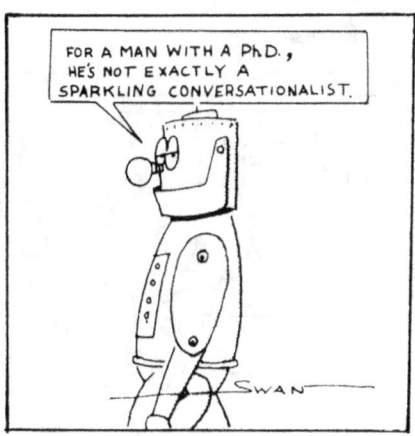

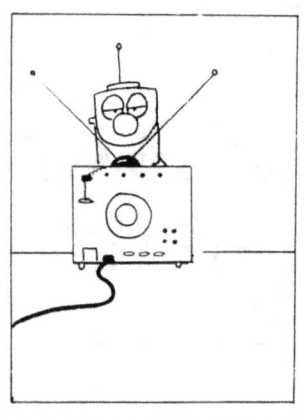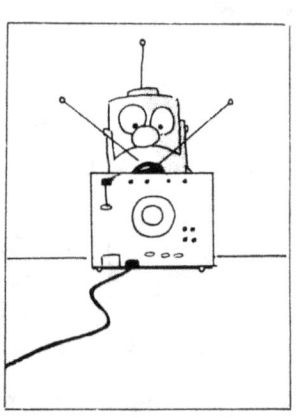

"Cold screwdriver, huh?"

"Did you see that movie about the robots that kill their programmers and take over the world? I laughed all the way through it!"

INSIDE JOKES

"Good morning, this is account number 35-0021-1973C. I'd like to be connected to my computer."

"I know it's been three days since installation, as soon as we find the OFF-ON switch you can start operations."

"Try to look like a computer."

"Sure it looks impressive ... but can it produce Snoopy printouts?"

"My money and patience have come to an end for your stupid project, Dr. Janis. As you insisted, all patent rights revert to you. What good is going back into time, anyway?"

"Why, in case it overflows, of course."

"I'd like you to meet Mr. Headly, he's a cyborg."

"He says that reminds him of the good old days."

"I'd be glad to put your information into layman's language, Mr. Turner, but I don't know any layman's language."

"It's our new self-programming terminal."

"If it's so smart, how come it ain't rich?"

"Good Grief! It's sprung a leak!!"

"Quick, Charlie! How much is 27 minus 6?"

"I'm afraid our computer is busy right now, sir. Would you like to speak with a human being?"

"He folded all cards."

"Fred's at that awkward stage between being replaced by a computer and collecting social security."

HARBAUGH'S HA HA'S

"He said he could fix it in half the time it was taking me, so I let him try..."

"...you thought it needed jazzed up?!!"

"You mean to tell me you spent 3 days in the think tank and all you thought of was strawberry ice-cream?!"

"I understand you set a new frisbee record with one of our tape reels..."

"You forgot to tell him it's an antique computer, ... he thinks it's ours..."

"Pi!! That's the quantity I forgot to factor in!!!"

"...oh, working on a 50 million dollar expansion program, ...what are you doing dear?"

"...our sales manager said when I finished this you'd say, 'Wow!, what a terrific idea'."

"Nevermind the Ho, Ho, Ho's..."

"He wants to see you about your tricky mailer, ... the one where the giant component pops out..."

"...I asked him to write a program language during his lunch hour..."

"...why didn't you tell me he had tennis elbow before I shook his hand?"

"You mean it's going to take two of those just to replace Hartwell?"

"Just a minute... we need TWO of them!"

HARD(WARE) SELL

"This is our finest economy model. It runs on just peanuts a day."

"Now this model is an extremely popular model - especially with our salesmen, because we get an exceptionally high commission if we unload them..."

"Gosh! How can you afford to sell a computer at that price?!"

"I figure it will pay for itself in the money we'd save on chalk."

"No charge at all to process these questions, ... the answers will be $850 an inch, though!"

"C'mon, everybody — let's hear it for the computer repairman!"

"Where did you learn to debug a program, Haverstraw?"

THIS DOES NOT ZAP! COMPUTE

"I can fix it, but I'll have to bring my shop here."

"I'll bet you 10 bucks it's Mrs. Platt's form again."

"It doesn't compute!"

"...why this is terrible! —— unless, of course, he comes up with the right answer to the malfunction.........!"

"This always works on my TV at home."

"It does the work of 50 girls, but you need 51 men to service it."

"Now the final assembled product is tested by this machine. That instrument checks the testing machine which in turn is tested by this system, then..."

"Of course, the hexical jackshaft limiter relay might possibly stick, preventing the coaxial copasolerator from actuating ... in which case, give it a kick."

"You didn't call the central data bank at all ... you called Dial-A-Joke didn't you?"

ONE ON ONE

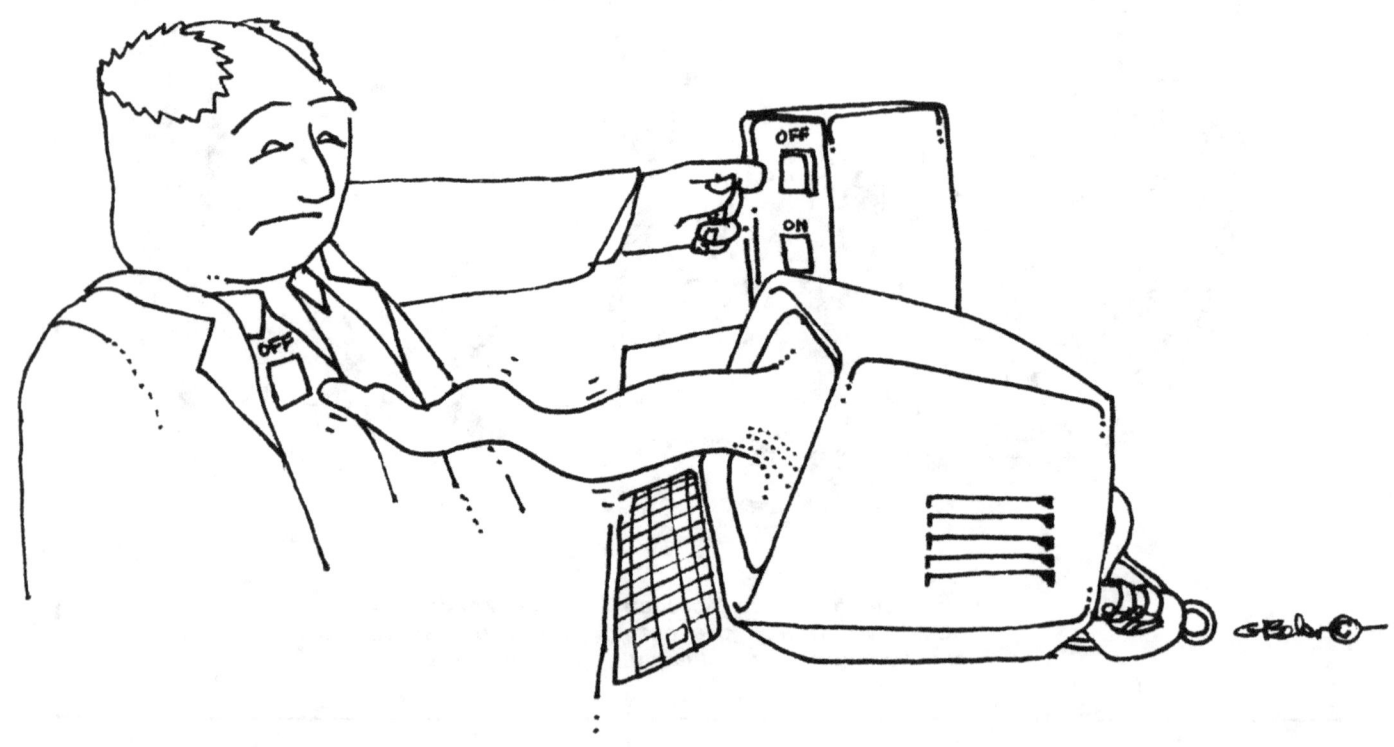

"Same to you."

"Had a bad weekend too, eh?"

"Oh yeah!"

"You're keeping something from me!!"

"Why did you turn off my power? I paid my bill. See? Here's my canceled check."

"Forgive me, Betty, forgive me! I'm sorry I kicked you in the side panel..."

"I can use base ten, and you can't."

"Give you Boardwalk?! Are you crazy?!"

SWAN'S CIRCUS

"The pulse amplifier's connected to the photomultiplier, the photomultiplier's connected to the........."

"It makes everything as easy as 3.1415926..."

"But you distinctly said to dump the files."

"And where were you when the FORTRAN hit the fan?"

"You're a hard worker, punctual, dedicated and the computer can't figure your little game."

"Turning off all the switches before you lock up doesn't include the LSI circuits!"

"You've got to stop asking it moot questions, Harry."

"You can't *quit right in the middle of an operational stress analysis!*"

IT'S ONLY HUMAN!

"So, it made a mistake. It's only human!"

"I'll have a ham on rye, and he'll have an incremental plotter with all the input options."

"It threw up when I programmed it to select the most honest political candidate."

"I fed our 'Delicacy Supreme' recipe into the computer... and he ate it!"

"It says we forgot to say 'May I'."

"It wants us to call in another computer for a consultation."

"The attendance at Sunday's game will be 64,837... but that's only a ballpark figure!"

"It's very impatient ... between questions, it doodles."

"I've found the trouble. The other computers are passing the work to number 12."

"About our prospects for that merger, it says: 'You have a snowball's chance in...'"

"If I asked it the wrong question, why did it answer?"

"There seems to be a mix-up in the tapes. I keep getting Guy Lombardo."

"It says the number you dialed is not a working number."

"I've been getting a lot of complaints about this computer, Baxter. I want to see both of you in my office!"

"It gives the answer as 12,621,859.007. But, it says it's just a hunch."

"...And when I hit 'Gently Down the Stream,' you come in with 'Row, Row, Row your Boat.'"

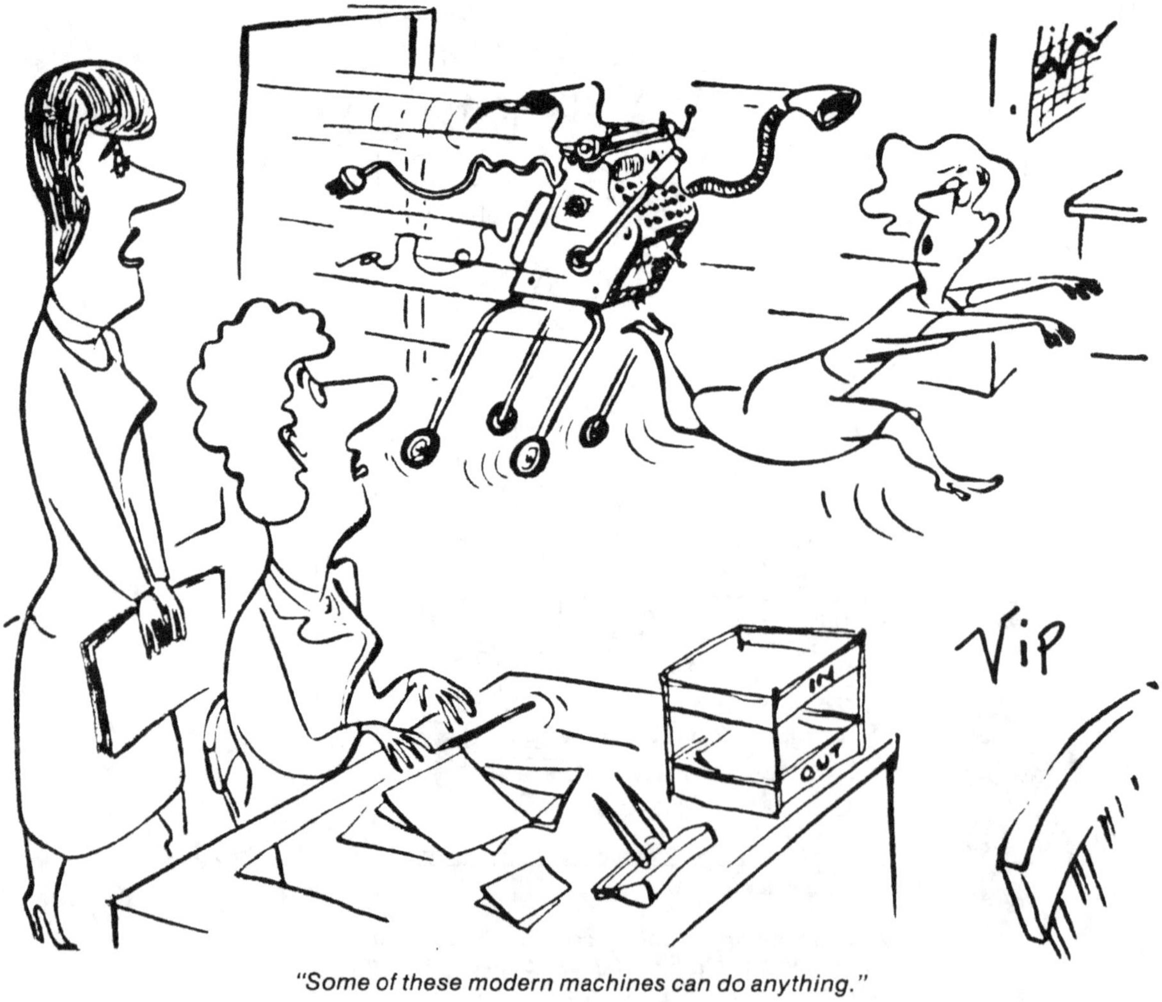

"Some of these modern machines can do anything."

SOLO CIRCUITRY

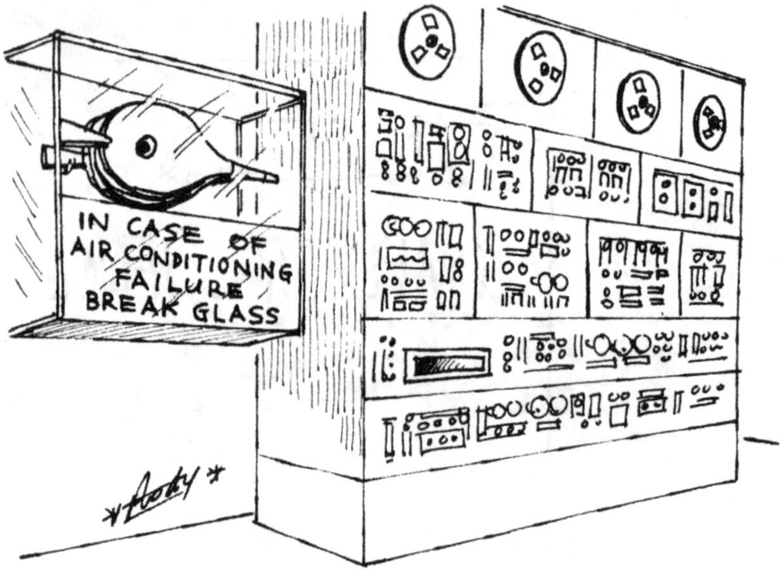

JOHNS' JOKES

"Uh ... about this loaner you sent us while our computer is being repaired..."

"Now, who are you going to believe... a forty year old mathematician or a two year old computer?"

"Let me begin by saying the computer was old and probably due to be replaced anyway."

"Our next speaker will talk on the subject of 'the pitfalls of electronic funds transfer systems'."

"C.J., find B.W. on the P.D.Q. and tell him two V.I.P.'s from I.B.M. and N.C.R. want to discuss the D.P.M.A. on the Q.T. with the E.D.P. and E.A.M. managers ... O.K.?"

"That's the third paragraph you've started with 'according to our computer'."

"Johnson, I hear you don't trust our new computer-based environmental control system."

"Well, let's see if the front office thinks THIS one is simple enough to operate!"

"What's wrong with his asking you for a date?... He's only thirty-four."

"What do you think of that, Mr. Genius?!"

www.ingramcontent.com/pod-product-compliance
Lightning Source LLC
Chambersburg PA
CBHW080921170526
45158CB00008B/2190